MW00848693

PRAYING WITH SAINTS AND SINNERS

Fr. Paul Brendan Murray, OP

Preface by Pope Francis

NOTES ON PRAYER

Volume 4

Our Sunday Visitor
Huntington, Indiana

Copyright © Dicastery for Evangelization 2024
Palazzo San Pio X, Via della Conciliazione, 5 00120 Città del Vaticano
www.pcpne.va; www.iubilaeum2025.va
Published 2024 by Our Sunday Visitor, Inc.

Scripture quotations are from *The ESV® Bible (The Holy Bible, English Standard Version®)*, copyright © 2001 by Crossway, a publishing ministry of Good News Publishers. Used by permission. All rights reserved.

Our Sunday Visitor Publishing Division
Our Sunday Visitor, Inc.
200 Noll Plaza
Huntington, IN 46750
1-800-348-2440

ISBN: 978-1-63966-274-6 (Inventory No. T2939)
eISBN: 978-1-63966-275-3
LCCN: 2024948664

Cover and interior design: Amanda Falk
Cover art: Adobestock

OSV extends thanks to the Catholc Truth Society for its collaboration in producing this book.

Printed in the United States of America

Contents

To my brother,
Myles

Preface by Pope Francis

———

Prayer is the breath of faith, its most proper expression. It's like a silent cry that comes out from the heart of whoever trusts and believes in God. It's not easy to find words to express this mystery. How many definitions of prayer we can gather from the saints and masters of spirituality, as well as from the reflections of theologians! Nevertheless, it is always and only in the simplicity of those who live prayer that prayer finds expression. The Lord, moreover, warned us that, when we pray, we must not waste words, deluding ourselves that thus we will be heard. He taught us rather to prefer silence and to entrust ourselves to the Father, who knows the kind of things we need even before we ask for them (see Mt 6:7–8).

The Ordinary Jubilee of 2025 is already at the door. How to prepare ourselves for this event, so important for the life of the Church, if not by means of prayer? The year 2023 was set aside for a rediscovery of the conciliar teachings, contained especially in the four constitutions of the Second Vatican Council. It is a way of keeping alive the mandate that the Fathers gathered at the council wished to place in our hands, so that by means of its implementation, the Church might recover its youthful face and proclaim, in a language adapted to the men and women of our time, the beauty of the Faith.

Now is the time to prepare for a year that will be dedicated entirely to prayer. In our own time the need is being felt more and more strongly for a true spirituality capable of responding to the great questions which confront us every day of our lives, questions caused by a global scenario that is far from serene. The ecological-economic-social crisis aggravated by the recent pandemic; wars, especially the one in Ukraine, which sow death, destruction, and poverty; the culture of indifference and waste that tends to stifle aspirations for peace and solidarity and keeps God at the margins of personal and social life. ... These phenomena combine to bring about a ponderous atmosphere that holds many people back from living with joy and serenity. What we need, therefore, is that our prayer should rise up with greater insistence to the Father so that he will listen to the voice of those who turn to him, confident of being heard.

This year dedicated to prayer is in no way intended to affect the initiatives which every particular Church considers it must plan for in its own daily pastoral commitment. On the contrary, it aims to recall the foundation on which the various pastoral plans should be developed and find consistency. This is a time when, as individuals or communities, we can rediscover the joy of praying in a variety of forms and expressions. A time of consequence enabling us to increase the certainty of our faith and trust in the intercession of the Virgin Mary and the saints. In short, a year in which we can have the experience almost of a "school of prayer," without taking anything for granted (or at cut-rate), especially with regard to our way of praying, but making our own, every day, the words of the disciples when they asked Jesus: "Lord, teach us to pray" (Lk 11:1).

In this year we are invited to become more humble and to leave space for the prayer that flows from the Holy Spirit. It is he who knows how to put into our hearts and onto our lips the right words so that we will be heard by the Father. Prayer in the Holy Spirit is what unites us with Jesus and allows us to adhere to the will of the Father. The Spirit is the interior Teacher who indicates the way to follow. Thanks to him the prayer of even just one person can become the prayer of the entire Church, and vice versa. There is nothing like prayer according to the Spirit to make Christians feel united as the one family of God. It is God who knows how to recognize everyone's needs and how to make those needs become the invocation and intercession of all.

I am certain that bishops, priests, deacons, and catechists will find more effective ways this year of placing prayer as the basis of the announcement of hope which the 2025 Jubilee intends to make resonate in this troubled time. For this reason, the contribution of consecrated persons will be of great value, particularly communities of contemplative life. I hope that in all the shrines of the world, privileged places for prayer, initiatives should be increased so that every pilgrim can find an oasis of serenity and return with a heart filled with consolation. May prayer, both personal and communal, be unceasing, without interruption, according to the will of the Lord Jesus (see Lk 18:1), so that the kingdom of God may spread, and the Gospel reach every person seeking love and forgiveness.

As an aid for this Year of Prayer, some short texts have been produced which, with their simple language, will make possible entry into the various dimensions of prayer. I thank the authors for their contribution and willingly place into your hands these "notes" so that everyone can rediscover the beauty of trusting in the Lord with humility and joy. And don't forget to pray also for me.

Vatican City
September 27, 2023

Franciscus

Introduction

———

The saints whose writings on prayer and meditation are explored in this book are among the most celebrated in the great spiritual tradition. They know, in depth, of the light and fire of which they speak. Page after page of their writings attain to levels of vision and understanding which are remarkable. The principal focus of the present work is not, however, on the higher states and stages of contemplative prayer. The aim is something far more modest — namely, to discover what help the great saints can offer those of us who desire to make progress in the life of prayer, but who find ourselves being constantly deflected from our purpose, our tentative efforts undermined perhaps most of all by human weakness.

One of the things we discover in the stories of the Christian saints, and it's a striking paradox, is that they learn how to pray, at least in part, from the witness of a certain number of celebrated sinners. Thus in the Second Way of Prayer in the Nine Ways of Prayer of Saint Dominic, for example, we witness the saint humbly repeating the publican's prayer from Saint Luke's Gospel: "God, be merciful to me a sinner!" (Lk 18:13).[1] Likewise, St. Teresa of Ávila, speaking of those who attain to the highest mansion of all in *The Interior Castle*, notes that they never lose contact with the humble spirit of the publican. Overwhelmed by the radiance and majesty of God and by the thought of their own human weakness, they sometimes "go about, like the publican, without daring to lift up their eyes."[2]

It was the publican, we are informed in Saint Luke's Gospel, not the Pharisee, who went home acquitted of his sins (see 18:13–14). Are we to take it, then, that when he walked away, he was completely unaware of the success of his prayer? On this question, with wry good humor, the Dominican Vincent McNabb remarks:

> The publican did not know he was justified. If you had asked him, "Can you pray?" he would have said, "No, I cannot pray. I was thinking of asking the Pharisee. He seems to know all about it. I could only say I was a sinner. My past is so dreadful. I cannot imagine myself praying. I am better at stealing."[3]

In the New Testament, no sinner's prayer made a greater impact than the bold appeal of the Good Thief on the Hill of Calvary: "Jesus, remember me when you come into your kingdom" (Lk 23:42). The reply Jesus gave was so swift, so unexpected, it must have pierced the man through with a wild, wondrous hope: "Today you will be with me in paradise" (v. 43). Elsewhere, in the tradition, we can find prayers similar to the stark appeal made here by the Good Thief, prayers born out of need and desperation but which, unknown to those who make them — the sinners and "thieves" of this world — capture and steal the heart of Christ Jesus.

Of all the examples I've come upon over the years of sinners at prayer, by far the most striking is a prayer composed by an anonymous monk of the early Church. It's a humble prayer, a naked prayer, a prayer one can certainly describe as desperation, but it's a prayer that is, at the same time, full of hope in God's mercy. And it's so candid, so bold, so touchingly honest, it always makes me smile when I read it. The stark, urgent appeal of the prayer is as sharp and alive now as it was centuries ago, when first composed:

> Lord, whether I want it or not, save me, because dust and ashes that I am, I love sin. But you are God almighty, so stop me yourself. If you have pity on the just, that's not much, or if you save the pure, because they are worthy of your mercy. Show the full splendor of your mercy in me. Reveal in me your love for men and women, because this poor man has no other refuge but you.[4]

The four chapters of this small book focus on the work of four saints, two men and two women. Here, in the order in which the work is addressed, are the names

11

and dates of the four saints: Augustine of Hippo, 354–430; Teresa of Ávila, 1515–82; Thomas Aquinas, 1225–74; Thérèse of Lisieux, 1873–97. All four are highly revered within the tradition, and all of them are named and acknowledged as Doctors of the Church. Their writings are remarkable for the revelation they contain of an achieved divine intimacy and friendship with God. But no less remarkable is the striking humility and poverty of spirit with which these saints turn spontaneously to God for help. Often, we find them at prayer raising their voices with the urgency of desire and the humble, illumined hope of sinners like the Good Thief and the publican.

The saints, it soon becomes clear, are human beings like us. That's why they can offer people still struggling with weakness such great compassion and encouragement. However, the remarkable sanctity of their lives remains a stark, unignorable challenge to our mediocrity. In their daring, prayerful, dedicated surrender to God, they have allowed their lives to be transformed by grace, and allowed the radiance, strength, power, and beauty of Christ to shine through their human weakness.

Augustine of Hippo at Prayer

―――――

Have pity on me and heal me, for you see that
I have become a problem to myself.
(*Confessions*, Bk 10, 33)

"I am most devoted to Saint Augustine," Teresa of Ávila writes in *The Book of Her Life*. The reason — the main reason — she offers to account for this devotion is "because he had been a sinner." That's a rather startling declaration, but Teresa goes on at once to explain: "I derived great comfort from those saints who have sinned and yet whom the Lord has drawn to himself. I thought that I could obtain help from them and that, as the Lord had pardoned them, he might pardon me."[5]

The *Confessions*, Augustine's most celebrated work, reveals with unsparing candor the nature of the weakness, the sin, which so plagued the saint as a young man:

> Bodily desire, like a morass, and adolescent sex welling up within me exuded mists which clouded over and obscured my heart so that I could

not distinguish the clear light of true love from the murk of lust. Love and lust together seethed within me … they swept me away over the precipice of my body's appetites and plunged me in a whirlpool of sin. (Bk 2, 2)[6]

Although Augustine longed to be free of this obsession with sex, nevertheless he recoiled from the prospect of being deprived of the fierce pleasure, the lust, which imprisoned him. With searing honesty, he turns to God and exclaims:

O Lord, you were setting me before my own eyes so that I could see how sordid I was, how deformed and squalid. … As a youth I had prayed to you for chastity, and said: "Give me chastity and continence, but not yet." For I was afraid that you would answer my prayer at once and cure me too soon of the disease of lust, which I wanted satisfied not quelled. (Bk 8, 7)

Right up to the actual moment of his conversion Augustine finds himself in a turmoil of indecision:

This was the nature of my sickness. I was in torment, reproaching myself more bitterly than ever as I twisted and turned in my chain. I hoped that my chain might be broken once and for all, because it was only a small thing that held me now. All the same it held me. … The closer I came to the moment, which was to mark the great change in me, the more I shrank from it in horror. (Bk 8, 11)

Then, a few moments later, from a nearby house, Augustine hears "the singsong voice of a child," repeating a simple refrain: "Take it and read. Take it and read." Choosing to interpret this as a divine summons, Augustine takes up his "book of Scripture." The first passage on which his gaze falls hits him like a bolt of lightning: "Not in orgies and drunkenness, not in sexual immorality and sensuality, not in quarreling and jealousy. But put on the Lord Jesus Christ, and make no provision for the flesh, to gratify its desires" (Rom 13:13–14). Augustine is at once pierced through by grace, his mind freed from all doubt, his heart flooded by a new radiant "light of confidence" (Bk 8, 12).

Confessions, composed between 397 and 401, is a single work consisting of thirteen books. The title of the work refers both to a confession of faults and to a confession of praise, an affirmation of trust and belief in the living God. No work of this kind had ever appeared in history before. It lays bare the inner heart of an individual man in search of God, but it is not a straightforward work of autobiography. In fact, from first page to last, it reads as a meditation addressed directly to God. How to explain this phenomenon? How to account for this new dynamic form of personal biography so strangely, so unexpectedly studded with prayers?

1. Augustine's discovery of the psalms

"How they set me on fire with love of you."
(*Confessions*, Bk 9, 4)

It was when Augustine was at Cassiciacum that the psalms first made their impact. One psalm in particular, Psalm 4, caught the young convert's attention. The prayer begins: "When I call on your name, listen to me, O God … have pity on me now and hear my prayer!" Reading these words in the presence of God, Augustine was profoundly shaken: "I quivered with fear, yet at the same time I was aglow with hope, rejoicing in your mercy, my Father" (see Bk 9, 4). From that time on Augustine became a passionate reader of the psalms, which no doubt explains why we find them quoted repeatedly in the *Confessions*. "How I cried out to you," he exclaims, "when I read those psalms! How they set me on fire with love of you! I was burning to echo them to all the world, if only I could" (ibid.).

This desire, in time, took the form of an extra-ordinary commentary on the psalms, the *Ennarationes* (*Expositions*).[7] Augustine worked on the commentary for nearly thirty years. It is by far his longest and most comprehensive work. Like the *Confessions* it contains many memorable prayers of Augustine. But it contains also a treasure of wisdom that's not found in the *Confessions* — namely, an in-depth series of teachings about prayer which finds almost no parallel in the tradition.

Augustine, struck by a brief phrase in Psalm 50 — "*Let me teach your ways to sinners*" — exclaims at once, "I am myself an ex-sinner, and as an ex-sinner, let me teach sinners" (*Expositions of the Psalms*, vol. 2, 425). In countless ways Augustine found his own life mirrored in the psalms, and he encouraged others to make the same discovery. Reflecting on Psalm 123, for example, he wrote: "Listen as though you were hearing yourselves. Listen as though you were looking at your own reflection in the mirror of the Scriptures" (vol. 6, 45).

The intense, restless way the psalms move from one level of discourse to another, their bold naming and exploration of human fears, joys, sorrows, and cravings, found in the soul of the young Augustine a strong and immediate echo. Poring over one psalm after another, he began to feel recognized, interpreted, understood. What's more, he discovered that reading the psalms, praying the psalms, was transformative, not only leading his mind to new levels of understanding, but also healing some of his heart's deepest wounds. That's why, in his commentary on Psalm 30, he offers this advice: "If the psalm is praying, pray yourselves; if it is groaning, you groan, too; if it is happy, rejoice; if it is crying out in hope, you hope as well; if it expresses fear, be afraid. Everything written here is like a mirror held up to us" (vol. 1, 347).

Augustine was convinced that the voice we hear in the psalms is not only that of the psalmist but also, on occasion, that of Christ Jesus: "He prays for us as our priest; he prays in us as our head; he is prayed to by us as our God. So, we must recognize our voices in him and his voices in us" (on Psalm 85, vol. 4, 220). The psalms should gradually begin to impact on every level of our being. "Not only," Augustine declares, "must your voice sing God's praises, but your actions must keep in tune with your voice" (on Psalm 146, vol. 6, 421).

And again, in a similar vein, he remarks: "Do you want your praise to be delightful to God? Do not allow your good singing to be drowned by the din of your bad morals" (ibid.).

2. A voice of encouragement

"Let him be your healing, who was willingly wounded for you."

(*Expositions*, on Psalm 42, vol. 2, 263)

Often the guilt which sinners feel can be so heavy they find it almost impossible to believe that God will forgive their many faults. Augustine, based on his own experience, understood this very well. That's why he takes the trouble to quote these lines from Psalm 33: "Draw near to him and receive his light, and you will not be put to shame" (vol. 2, 32). But hearing this declaration, the sinner, Augustine surmises, will most likely find it hard to credit. Hence, the dialogue that follows:

How can I draw near to him? I am laden with grave offenses, burdened with serious sins. The

foulest crimes raise their clamor from my conscience. How can I dare to approach God? How?
Quite easily, if you have first humbled yourself
in repentance. But I am ashamed to repent, you
answer. Well then, draw near to him and you
will be illumined, and then your face will not
be forced to blush with shame. ... Cry out in
poverty, cry as a poor person, and the Lord will
listen. (ibid.)

In another place Augustine allows us, once again, to
hear the voice of the troubled sinner. Citing, first, the
entreaty from Psalm 129, "Out of the depths I have
cried to you, Lord; / O Lord, hear my voice," Augustine writes: "Where does this cry come from? From
the deep. Who utters it? The sinner. Why can he hope
to be heard? Because Christ who came to do away
with sin, has given hope even to a sinner sunk in the
deep" (vol. 6, 128). But, for such tremendous hope to
enter deep into the bloodstream and fire the heart,
time is needed. That explains the dramatic back and
forth dialogue which, on an occasion such as this, can
take place inside the mind of the sinner:

"Do you, an unjust sinner, dare to ask God for
anything? Do you dare hope that you will enjoy
some contemplation of God, you weakling, you
with your unclean heart? Yes, I do dare, I answer,
because ... I don't rely on myself but on God's
pledge." (on Psalm 26, 2, vol. 1, 280–81)

The period directly after conversion is a time of manifest blessing and joy. The individual discovers that, with God's help, he or she can begin to live virtuously, and that brings with it a great sense of well-being. But this new ease of spirit can sometimes be undermined by complacency or presumption.

"After repentance," Augustine writes, "when such a person has begun to lead a good life, he still needs to be careful not to attribute that good conduct to his own strength" (on Psalm 93, vol. 4, 391). The individual needs, in other words, to be humble, not proud. For it is to "the little ones," Augustine notes, commenting on Psalm 118, that God imparts his "light and understanding." "What is meant here by '*little ones*'?" Augustine asks. And he replies, "Surely people who are humble and weak" — in other words, people who are poor in spirit like the publican, not proud like the Pharisee (see, on Psalm 118, vol. 5, 472).

At this point, in his commentary, Augustine begins to sound — amazing to report — like St. Thérèse of Lisieux. Thus we hear him declare, in the same section of *Expositions*: "A weak person has no means of performing mighty feats, nor could a little one achieve great things; so the psalmist opened his mouth to confess that he could not do it of himself, and he drew in the Breath that would empower him to do it." The paradoxical aim of this process — the Gospel hope — is, Augustine explains, "to turn you from a great person to a little one" — that is, from an arrogant, self-justifying individual to someone truly humble and poor in spirit. Based on that vision, Augustine, with Thérèsian confidence, can boldly declare, "Let [us] all be little!"

———✵———

A near obsession in Augustine's writing is the theme of desire. "Think how powerful," he notes, "are the desires in human hearts. ... Everyone burns with desire." But then he adds, "There are precious few who can say to God, '*My soul is athirst for you*'" (on Psalm 62, vol. 3, 233). It is prayer which, more than anything else, enables an individual to leave the world of superficial distraction, descend to the root of desire, and there begin to *find delight in contemplating the Lord* (see *Ps 26*).

Augustine writes these radiant words: "If you want to be a lover of God, then, choose him from the bottom of your heart and with the utmost sincerity, love him with chaste longing, burn for him, thirst for him. You will find nothing better, nothing more joyful, nothing more lasting, than God. What could be more lasting than what lasts forever?" (on Psalm 85, vol. 4, 228-29). In all of Augustine's writings, perhaps the most moving, most compelling description of falling in love with God are these lines from the *Confessions*:

> Late, late, have I loved you, O Beauty ever ancient and ever new! You were within me, and I was in the world outside myself. I searched for you out-

side myself and, disfigured as I was, I fell upon the lovely things of your creation. You were with me, but I was not with you. ... You called me; you cried aloud to me; you broke my barrier of deafness. You shone upon me; your radiance enveloped me; you put my blindness to flight. You shed your fragrance about me; I drew breath and now I gasp for your sweet odor. I tasted you, and now I hunger and thirst for you. You touched me, and now I burn for your peace. (Bk 10, 27)

3. Augustine's ongoing conversion

"In our present state, how many unlawful pleasures brush against our minds!"
(on Psalm 146, vol. 6, 425)

The tenth book of the *Confessions*, which contains the celebrated "Late, late, have I loved you" passage, also contains other prayers no less eloquent of the newfound joy which Augustine now finds in contemplating God. We read, for example: "Sometimes you allow me to experience a feeling quite unlike my normal state, an inward sense of delight which, if it were to reach perfection in me, would be something not encountered in this life" (Bk 10, 40). Here, the remarkable history of Augustine's long journey to God would seem to have at last come to a serene and happy conclusion. By God's grace, the great sinner has become a great saint. The man once greatly afflicted by sensual temptation and human weakness now stands in the light and joy of God's presence.

It's certainly a positive and happy picture, and a true picture so far as it goes. But it is by no means the whole story. For, immediately after speaking about his contemplative experience of "inward delight," Augustine writes: "But my heavy burden of distress drags me down again to earth. Again, I become a prey to my habits, which hold me fast. My tears flow, but still I am held fast. Such is the price we pay for the burden of custom!" (ibid.). Reflecting on the post-conversion experience of Augustine, Pope Benedict XVI, no doubt having in mind passages such as the one just quoted, made a sharp and telling observation: "Saint Augustine, at the moment of his conversion, thought he had reached the heights of life with God. ... He then had to understand that the journey after conversion is still a journey of conversion."[8] What Augustine discovered, in his maturity, was that in the daily struggle to follow Christ we must learn to "accept our frailty but keep on going, not giving up, but moving forward and becoming converted ever anew" (Bk 10, 40).

When, on one occasion, Augustine was invited to give a series of talks at Carthage, his audience must have been stunned when they heard the great and famous bishop declare: "Here in this very city I led an evil life. I confess it. And just as I rejoice over God's grace in me, so for my evil past I — what? Shall I say 'grieve'?" Augustine's reply is immediate: "Certainly

… would that I had never been such! For I suffer torture in my thoughts; I have to struggle against evil suggestions; my conflict with the enemy who tempts me is a daily one, well-nigh an unceasing one."[9]

All human beings, even the great saints, according to Augustine, although they may not yield to the promptings of serious sin, experience, nevertheless, what he calls "the desires inspired by sin" (*Expositions*, on Psalm 118, vol. 5, 352). And that's why he is not shy of declaring, "Even people, who are walking in the ways of the Lord, pray: *Forgive us our sins*" (ibid.). To both saint and sinner, therefore, Augustine makes bold to say: "You are human!"

You may be a just person, you're human; you may be a lay person, you're human; a monk or a nun, you're human; a clergyman, you're human; a bishop, you're human; an apostle, you're human. Listen to the words of an apostle: *If we say we have no sin, we are deceiving ourselves.* Who said it? That one … [is] John the Evangelist whom the Lord Christ loved above the rest, who reclined on his bosom; that's the one who says, "*If we say.*" Not "if you say that you have no sin," but *if we say that we have no sin, we are deceiving ourselves, and the truth is not in us.* He included himself in the fault in order to be included in the pardon.[10]

Regarding those faults which "arise from our former habits of sin," St. John Newman remarks with a straightforwardness and candor worthy of Augustine:

We cannot rid ourselves of sin when we would; though we repent, though God forgives us, yet it remains in its power over our souls, in our habits, and in our memories. It has given a color to our thoughts, words, and works; and though, with many efforts, we would wash it out from us, yet this is not possible except gradually.[11]

The struggle for holiness of life, for purity of life, is in no way weakened or diminished by this honest and sane observation. As we confront the trials and struggles of the spiritual life, both saints encourage us not to become frozen in fear at the thought of our human weakness. Thus Augustine, commenting on the line, "*Why are you sorrowful, O my soul, and why do you disquiet within me?*" writes, "Why be afraid about your sins, when you know you have not the strength to avoid them all?" (on Psalm 42, vol. 2, 263). He then cites the line, "*Hope in the Lord for I will confess to him*," declaring that the encouragement of these words effect "some healing at once," and in time the remaining sins can be "purged by faithful confession" (ibid.).

Passages such as these in Augustine's writings are manifestly helpful and encouraging, but it is the witness of his life that offers the greatest hope to the struggling sinner. And hope is what Augustine prayed for so often and so movingly:

O Lord our God, let *the shelter of your wings*

give us hope. Protect us and uphold us. You will be the support that upholds us from childhood till the hair on our heads is gray. When you are our strength, we are strong, but when our strength is our own, we are weak. … Let us come home at last to you, O Lord, for fear that we be lost. For in you our good abides, and it has no blemish, since it is yourself. (*Confessions*, Bk 4, 16)

In this brief chapter we have been able to touch on only one or two themes in Augustine's work. But the voice of the saint, although it comes to us from a world that is long gone, speaks with bold honesty and such weight of experience that it still, today, carries an illumined and eminently practical message for all those attempting to pray and follow the path of the Gospel. "When I read St. Augustine's writings," Pope Benedict XVI remarked, "I do not get the impression that he is a man who died more or less 1,600 years ago; I feel he is like a man of today, a friend, a contemporary, who speaks to me, who speaks to us, with his fresh and timely faith."[12]

Augustine of Hippo is not simply a great author; he is a living witness of what he teaches and preaches. That's why, with a force and eloquence unmatched in the tradition, he can alert both saints and sinners to what Pope Benedict calls the humble, necessary grace of "ongoing conversion."[13]

Teresa of Ávila at Prayer

---

*Recover, my God, the lost time by giving me
grace in the present.*

("*Soliloquies*," 4, Collected Works)[14]

1. A portrait of the saint

Over the last four hundred years attempts have been
made by artists, historians, and theologians to produce
— in either words or color — a portrait of St. Teresa of
Ávila. One portrait was completed during Teresa's lifetime. The artist, an earnest but rather mediocre paint-
er, was an Italian friar called Juan de la Miseria. We
find the execution of the painting described in some
detail by Teresa's great Carmelite friend Jerónimo
Gracián: "Fra Juan told her to put on the kind of expression he wanted to see on her face and scolded her
when she could no longer keep herself from laughing
and started to lose the expression."[15] The result, not
surprisingly, was a disappointment. Despite Juan's best
efforts to paint, and Teresa's brave efforts to sit still,
"the likeness," in Gracián's opinion, "showed none of
the natural charm and grace of the holy mother's expression." Teresa herself, when she saw the painting,
remarked with quick, exuberant wit: "God forgive

you, Brother Juan, first you plague *the* life out of me and then … you paint me looking so ugly and bleary-eyed!"

Fortunately, over the centuries, few of the efforts of artists and theologians to portray Teresa have been as unhappy in execution as the painting by Fra Juan. I sometimes wonder, however, if Teresa would be able to recognize herself and her work in some of the earnest, heavy tomes that have been written about her unique spiritual journey. But rather than place all the blame here on the theologians, it must be acknowledged that any attempt by commentators to define the figure of Teresa and her work is likely to meet with failure. So distinctive, so original is her spirit, character, personality, humor, and holiness, that Teresa quite simply defies definition.

By the force of her character, by the boldness of her activity as a foundress, and by her remarkable ability to speak and to write in depth on the subject of prayer, Teresa astonished her contemporaries. But not everyone was impressed. Certain people, far from rejoicing in her extraordinary energy and giftedness, openly opposed the work she was doing and her teaching. They insisted that, as a woman, she had no right to go outside the enclosure, invoking for their authority the statement of Saint Paul in First Corinthians that women "are not permitted to speak" (1 Cor 14:34).

Teresa, troubled that in some way she may not be

doing God's will, turned to God in prayer. The answer she received, in private revelation, was as piercing and sudden as a double-edged sword: "Tell them they shouldn't follow just one part of Scripture but that they should look at other parts and ask them if they can by chance tie my hands."[16]

Centuries after her death, Teresa was somehow still able to surprise the Church and the world. Prior to 1970, no woman had ever been named a Doctor of the Church. That's why, in 1967, the section on "Doctor of the Church" in the *New Catholic Encyclopedia* noted that "no woman is likely to be named Doctor of the Church because of the link between this title and the teaching office of the Church which is limited to males."[17] A mere three years later, however, Pope Paul VI included Teresa among the Doctors of the Church. He spoke of her as not only a remarkable teacher of "the secrets of prayer" but also as a "writer of great genius, a mistress of spiritual life, an incomparable contemplative."[18] If we ask ourselves how it was that Teresa acquired the "secrets" of prayer in such depth, Paul VI gives us the answer in one telling sentence: "She had the privilege and the merit to get to know these secrets through experience."

Perhaps the most iconic image of Teresa is the celebrated statue of the saint by Gian Lorenzo Bernini. Standing over Teresa, as she swoons in ecstasy, we see a brilliant young angel holding in his right hand a fiery sword which, moments earlier, it is imagined, he had plunged deep into the heart of the visionary. This dramatic encounter with the angel derives from an episode described by Teresa. When, finally, the sword with its tip of fire was pulled out, Teresa writes, "I thought he was carrying off with him the deepest part of me; and he left me all on fire with great love of God."[19] The Teresa whom we are witnessing here is the mystic saint, the seraphic Teresa, a woman of prayer so graced with extraordinary visions and ecstasies that her account of them can leave the readers of her work breathless with wonder. But Teresa's work — her writings — also reveal another Teresa, a figure so humble, so human, so fallible at times in her early efforts to concentrate at the time of prayer, it is hard to credit they are one and the same person. Here the focus of our attention is on this earlier Teresa.

2. A humble method of prayer for unruly minds

*"Now, that you might so walk along this path
that you do not go astray at the beginning, let us deal a
little with how this journey must begin."*

(*The Way of Perfection*, ch. 20, 3)[20]

To the young Teresa an impressive amount of information was readily available about prayer. It was several years, however, before she came to realize what was, for her, the best way forward. Writing in *The Way of Perfection* she notes that "there are many good books written by able people for those who have methodical minds and for souls that are experienced and can concentrate within themselves" (ch. 19, 1). But Teresa's mind was not of that type or character. She writes: "I suffered many years from the trial — and it is a very great one — of not being able to quiet the mind in anything" (ch. 26, 2). Far from being calm and methodical in her approach to prayer, Teresa was one of those people whose minds are "so scattered they are like wild horses no one can stop. Now they're running here, now there, always restless" (ch. 19, 2). And even "if they want to pause and think of God, a thousand absurdities, scruples, and doubts come to mind" (ch. 17, 3).

The method of prayer which, in time, Teresa developed to help her distracted mind focus on God involves two things. First, the recitation of a simple vocal prayer such as the Our Father, and, second, the practice of the presence of God. She writes: "This is the method of prayer I then used: since I could not reflect discursively with the intellect, I strove to represent Christ within me, and it did me greater good to represent him in those scenes where I saw him alone" (*The Book of Her Life*, ch. 9, 4). Based on knowledge gained from experience, Teresa offers the following advice: "If you speak, strive to remember that the One with whom you are speaking is present within. If you listen, remember that you are going to hear One who is very close to you" (*The Way of Perfection*, ch. 29, 7).

None of this, of course, will be easy at the beginning — far from it. But that does not hold Teresa back from declaring, "Get used to praying the Our Father with this recollection, and you will see the benefit before long" (ch. 29, 6). In a similar vein: "I only ask you to try this method, even though it may mean some struggle; everything involves struggle before the habit is acquired. But I assure you that, before long, it will be a great consolation for you to know that you can find this holy Father, whom you are beseeching, within you without tiring yourself" (ibid.).

3. Recovering the lost time

"Now, then, if the Lord put up with someone
as miserable as myself for so long a time ...
who, no matter how bad
they may be, has reason to fear?"
(*The Book of Her Life*, ch. 8, 8)

Teresa's journey to God is marked by a series of almost unimaginable wonders, swift flights of rapture, zones of stillness and quiet, visions of sublime beauty, wounds of ecstatic pain and joy. Over the years, perceptive scholars and commentators have reflected on the steps and stages of this high mystical journey and offered helpful and illuminating insights. But, here, our most immediate aim is on something more humble, more basic — namely, to discover the practical guidance which Teresa has to offer the disheartened individual who is finding the task of prayer difficult and unrewarding.

As a young nun, what Teresa dreaded more than anything else was the hour of meditation: "I was more anxious," she writes, "that the hour I had determined to spend in prayer be over than I was to remain there, and more anxious to listen for the striking of the clock than to attend to other good things" (*The Book of Her Life*, ch. 8, 7). What's more, so profound was the sadness she felt "on entering the oratory," she had to muster up "all her courage" to go through the door. What made the task so difficult was not simply the challenge of maintaining concentration in prayer but her pained awareness of the persistence of certain sins in her life. How could she presume to appear in the presence of the One whom she felt she was constantly betraying? Teresa writes, "I say courage for I do not know what would require greater courage among all the things there are in the world than to betray the King and know that he knows it and yet never leave his presence" (ch. 8, 2).

For more than "eighteen years," Teresa admits, this situation remained unresolved:

> I recount this so that one may understand how if the soul perseveres in prayer, in the midst of the sins, temptations, and failures of a thousand kinds … in the end, I hold as certain, the Lord will draw it forth to the harbor of salvation as —

now it seems — he did for me. May it please his
Majesty that I do not get lost again. (ch. 8, 4)

When Teresa looks back at the many lost opportuni-
ties she was given and reflects on the years spent seeking to avoid the presence of the One who was seeking her, what strikes her most forcibly is the reality of
God's patience:

> O my God, how infinitely good you are! … How
> true it is that you suffer those who will not suffer
> you to be with them? What a good friend you
> are, O my Lord, to comfort and endure them,
> and wait for them to rise to your condition, and
> yet in the meantime to be patient of the state
> they are in! You take into account, O Lord, the
> times they loved you, and for one moment of
> penitence forget all their offenses against you.
> This I have clearly seen in my own case, and I
> cannot see, O my Creator, why the whole world
> does not draw near to you in this bond of friend-
> ship.[21]

The mystical favors and consolations Teresa received
in prayer are among the things for which she is best
known, and Teresa was not in principle skeptical of
such phenomena. On the contrary, she believed that
favors of this kind had strengthened her faith and
her friendship with God. But Teresa never made the
mistake of equating such phenomena with the reality

of actual union with God. "The love of the Lord," she writes, "does not consist in these consolations and tendernesses which we so much desire and in which we find comfort, but in our serving him in justice, fortitude, and humility" (*The Life of Saint Teresa by Herself*, ch. 11, 81).

Not many Christian believers in this life will experience the extraordinary favors so vividly described by Teresa. But, with regard to experiencing in faith the living waters of prayer, with regard in other words to actual contemplative union with God, Teresa is happy to declare: "Behold, the Lord invites all!" (*The Way of Perfection*, ch. 19, 15). At the core, prayer for Teresa is something very simple: "a friendly intercourse and frequent solitary conversation with him who, we know, loves us" (*The Life of St. Teresa by Herself*, ch. 8, 63).

Those who wish to grow in prayer and contemplation must, as best they can, in Teresa's understanding, convert their lives to the standards of the Gospel. Addressing her fellow contemplatives in *The Interior Castle*, she writes: "It is necessary that your foundation consist of more than prayer and contemplation. If you do not strive for the virtues and practice them, you will always be dwarfs!" (The Seventh Dwelling Place, ch. 4, 9). This does not mean, however, that struggling sinners, until they have completely converted their lives, should be discouraged from praying. No, the opposite is the case, as Teresa came in time to understand. As a young nun, discouraged at one point by the persistence of certain sins in her life, she decided to give up praying altogether until she managed to control her weakness: "I never thought I would cease being determined to return to prayer — but I was waiting to be very purified of sin. Oh, how wrong was the direction I was going with this hope! The devil would have kept me hoping until judgment day" (*The Book of Her Life*, ch. 19, 11).

Teresa sought advice from a Dominican friar, Vicente Barrón, who actively encouraged her to continue her prayer and to receive the Eucharist. "He woke me from this sleep," Teresa writes, "and I began to return to my senses" (ch. 19, 12). It was a lesson Teresa never forgot. And that, no doubt, explains why so often in her writings we find Teresa urging those who have fallen back into sin never to give up the practice of prayer. No one, she declares, who has begun to practice prayer should become discouraged, thinking, if I fall back into sin, it will be better for me not to go on practicing prayer. On the contrary, Teresa insists, things will become much worse should prayer be abandoned. If, however, people keep faith with the practice of prayer, they can be confident that, in time, prayer will lead them safely to "the harbor of life" (ch. 19, 4).

Reflecting, on one occasion, on her own past life, Teresa was moved to exclaim: "Oh, how late have my desires been enkindled!" ("Soliloquies," 4, *Collected Works*, vol. 1, 446). She was thinking with regret on how long it had taken her to turn to God, while God had, for such a long time, been seeking to capture her attention. However, in spite of being painfully aware of such "time lost," and in spite of the fact, as she acknowledges, that people "usually say lost time cannot be recovered," Teresa, remembering Christ and the amazing strength and power of his compassion, makes bold to declare, "You, Lord, can win this time back again." And she prays: "O Lord, I confess your great power. If you are powerful, as you are, what is impossible for you who can do everything?" And again: "Although I am miserable, I firmly believe you can do what you desire." Greatly strengthened by this reflection, Teresa's prayer concludes: "Recover, my God, the lost time by giving me grace in the present … for if you want to you can do so."

Thomas Aquinas at Prayer

———

To you, O God, Fountain of Mercy, I come as a sinner.
("*The Prayer for Forgiveness,*" Piae Preces)[22]

1. A theologian on his knees

Best known for his profound and sober explorations in the fields of philosophy and theology, St. Thomas Aquinas's clear aim as a friar preacher was to draw others to Christ by doing all he could to communicate the saving wisdom of the Gospel. He had no desire whatsoever to draw attention to himself. That explains why, in his work, he studiously avoids using the word *I*. However, in the texts which have survived of Saint Thomas at prayer, we find the word *I* coming quite naturally to his lips. Reading these prayers, these *piae preces* ("pious prayers"), we are hearing or overhearing the personal, individual voice of a saint at prayer, and that is no small privilege:

> To you, O God, Fountain of Mercy,
> I come as a sinner,
> that you would deign to wash away my uncleanness.

O Sun of justice,
give sight to a blind man.
O Eternal Healer,
cure one who is wounded.
O King of Kings,
clothe the destitute.
O Mediator between God and Man,
restore the guilty.
O Good Shepherd,
lead back the stray.
Give, O God,
mercy to the wretched,
reprieve to the criminal,
life to the dead,
justification to the sinful,
and, to the hard of heart,
the anointing of grace.

To anyone who has not before now had the opportunity of reading some of the prayers attributed to the Angelic Doctor, these lines from *Prayer for Forgiveness (Oratio: pro peccatorum remissione)* may come as a surprise. Here, Aquinas is not writing as an astute and brilliant philosopher nor as a great and famous dogmatic theologian. He is instead humbly praying for the wounded, the blind, the destitute, the straying, the sinful, the hard of heart. And he is praying also for himself, "*me immundum*," a man *unclean*. But can this really be Thomas? Is he not acknowledged universally as a great saint, and are saints not distinguished from sinners by the perfect holiness of their lives? Holiness, yes, Thomas would agree, and "perfect," yes, provided this does not suggest "*all*-perfect." "All of us have some sin," Thomas notes in his lectures on Matthew's Gospel.[23] And, elsewhere, in a commentary on the Lord's Prayer, he remarks:

> There have been some so presumptuous as to assert that we could live in this world and, by our own unaided strength, avoid sin. But this has been given to none save Christ, who had the Spirit beyond all measure, and the Blessed Virgin who was full of grace and in whom there was no sin. … To no other saint has this been granted without their incurring at least venial sin. (*In Orationem Dominicam, expositio* no. 1082)

That the prayers attributed to Saint Thomas, the *Piae Preces*, were indeed most probably authored by Thomas has been the generally accepted view from the late Middle Ages until modern times. A. G. (Antonin) Sertillanges declared, in fact, that the *preces* deserve without question to be grouped "under the high signature" of Aquinas: "The depth and structure of these writings correspond so well with the doctrine, style, and natural movement of Thomistic thought that those readers most familiar with the works of Aquinas are those least liable to doubt the mark of Aquinas."[24] This conviction, regarding Thomas's authorship of the *preces*, although not shared by all scholars today, received notable encouragement in 1987 with the discovery that two of the prayers had been included in *The Life of St. Thomas Aquinas* by his contemporary William of Tocco and attributed to the holy saint.[25]

The first of these prayers, *Adoro Te Devote*, was composed by Thomas to assist his meditation when kneeling before Christ Jesus present in the Eucharist. It is generally acknowledged as the most truly profound and beautiful prayer ever composed by the saint. It begins:

> *Adoro te devote, latens veritas,*
> *te quae sub his formis vere latitas.*
> *Tibi se cor meum totum subicit,*
> *quia te contemplans totum deficit.*

> You, I devoutly adore, hidden Truth,
> you who, under these forms, are truly hidden.
> My whole heart submits itself to you for,
> in contemplating you, all else fails.

Thomas, while reflecting in the prayer on the challenge and mystery of belief, calls to mind two lowly Gospel figures: first, the Good Thief on the cross, and, second, Doubting Thomas. Being able, like them, to give voice to a faith both heartfelt and humble, he declares: "I pray the prayer of the dying thief." Turning then to his Incarnate Lord, with thoughtful and inspired confidence, he declares: "I do not see wounds, as Thomas

42

did, but I confess you as my God" (*Adoro Te Devote*).

What impresses throughout this prayer, but most particularly in the sixth stanza, is the direct personal voice of need and desire. Thomas begins the following stanza evoking the mythical story of the pelican which, because it had wounded itself in order to feed its young with its own lifeblood, had come to symbolize Christ's sacrificial love on the cross. Thomas's manifest longing to experience that redeeming love fully and personally is immediately striking. I know of no more humble, more moving statement of belief in all of Thomas's writings:

> *Pie pellicane, Jesu domine,*
> *me immundum munda tuo sanguine,*
> *cuius una stilla salvum facere,*
> *totum mundum posset omni scelere.*

> O kind Pelican, Lord Jesus,
> cleanse me, who am unclean in your blood,
> one drop of which would be enough to save
> the whole world of all its defilement.

2. Praying out of need

What is common to the stanza quoted above from *Adoro Te Devote,* and the stanzas cited earlier from the *Prayer for Forgiveness*, is that they are prayers of asking, are prayers of humble petition. Such prayers may seem like poor relations when compared with the vivid accounts of ecstasy and rapture we find reported in the lives and writings of the saints and mystics. But, for Saint Thomas, the prayer of asking — the prayer of petition — is at the very core of Christian prayer, and that remains true no matter how profound or mystical prayer may become.

But what about the other forms of Christian prayer, such as the prayer of quiet, the prayer of praise, and the prayer of thanksgiving? These are all genuine forms of Christian prayer, but they are not so essentially a part of the life of longing and need as is the prayer of petition. All of them, we can say, are rooted and grounded in petition. Thus, even in the prayer of praise, for example, we find an implicit acknowledgment of need, a prayer of need. God, the divine Object of praise is, at the same time, the Subject, the divine Spirit praying within us, interceding for us when we don't know how to pray or how to praise. By our own efforts alone, we can never hope to give adequate praise to the One who is "greater than all praise." The reality of our need is that profound. And so, Thomas, aware not only of prayer's extraordinary privilege and mystery, but aware also of the stark humility of spirit which it demands, goes so far as to declare, "It is fitting to praise God by God."[26]

Because Christian prayer quite often takes the form of asking God for help, it can be caricatured as a demeaning, slavish form of prayer, an activity which in some way undermines the dignity of the human person. But nowhere in Thomas's prayers of asking is there any hint of that. Take, for example, the magnificent *Prayer for Wise Ordering*, the second of the two *preces* which William of Tocco included in his biography of Thomas and attributed to the saint. The prayer is said by a man asking for an ever-deeper knowledge of God, and there is an urgency in the asking. But Thomas, although willing to disclose the depth of his need for grace, stands before God with an unmistakable sense of presence and sense of character. The adjectives he employs when attempting to describe the person he would most wish to become are revealing of the impressive integrity of spirit and character which, in considerable measure, he already possesses: "vigilant, noble, unconquered, free, and upright."

Give me, dearest God, a vigilant heart
which no distracting thought can lure away from you.

Give me a noble heart
which no unworthy desire can ever debase.

Give me an unconquered heart
which no tribulation can fatigue.

Give me a free heart
which no violent temptation can enslave.

Give me an upright heart
which no perverse intention can hold fast.[27]

3. Praying with confidence

At the close of the *Prayer for Wise Ordering*, among the graces which Thomas asks from God is the gift of confidence: "Grant me, Lord my God … perseverance in confidently waiting on you, and confidence in finally embracing you." *Confidence* — that's the word which, perhaps more than any other, highlights the distinctive character of Aquinas's prayer. Writing in *The Compendium of Theology*, he notes: "The confidence a human being has in God ought to be most certain."[28] In a similar vein, speaking to a packed church in Naples, Italy, on the Lord's Prayer, he declares, "Of all the things required of us when we pray, confidence is of great avail."[29] And then he adds, "For this reason … Our Lord, in teaching us how to pray, sets out before us those things which engender confidence in us, such as the loving kindness of a father, implied in the words *Our Father*." The Lord's Prayer Thomas describes as "the most perfect of all prayers" (*Summa Theologiae*, II, q. 83, ad 9). It is a prayer as simple as it is profound, in large part a prayer of petition. But also, Thomas points out, it is the liturgical prayer of the Mass. "In the Mass," he writes, "everything up to the consecration of the Body and Blood is 'entreaty.'"[30]

As human beings, because of weakness, we find it difficult to believe that we are truly loved by God. But Christ, as our mediator, was able, Thomas explains, "by the devotion of prayer to reach God at one extreme and, by mercy and compassion, to reach ourselves at the other."[31] In virtue of the Incarnation, Christ knew intimately, "through experience," what it was like to be weak and tempted. "*He himself was beset with weakness,*" Thomas explains, quoting Hebrews. He adds: "The reason for this is that he may have compassion on the weaknesses of others. This is the reason why the Lord permitted Peter to fall."

In prayer, if the prayer is honest, what is inevitably laid bare is our human need — our *miseria.* But also revealed, and of much greater importance, is the *misericordia,* the loving mercy and compassion of God. Worthy of note, in this context, is a luminous detail regarding the liturgy of the Mass which we find highlighted by Thomas. The texts used most often in the Mass, he notes, are the psalms composed by David (a man "who obtained pardon after sin") and the letters written by Paul (a man who likewise "obtained mercy") "so that, by these examples, sinners might be aroused to hope."[32]

As a scholar and a man of prayer, Saint Thomas was wholly dedicated to two things: the contemplation of God's Word and the proclamation of the Good News. His "wings" of contemplation, to use one of his own images, were those of "a dove" of contemplation, not those of "a raven."[33] His life of prayer and study was never for himself alone. He was a dove of kindness: His whole aim in life, unlike that of the selfish raven, was to serve the needs of others and bring to them the fruits of his contemplation. From several of the early witnesses of Thomas's life we hear reports of mystical phenomena such as visions, prophecy, and the gift of tears. But Thomas, with regard to the inner story of his own contemplative life, remains silent. His mysticism is undemonstrative, discreet. It finds expression not in fascinating psychological or psycho-spiritual experiences, but rather in a lifetime's prayerful study of the Word of God and in inspired works of wisdom.

One of the finest of these works is Part Two of the *Compendium of Theology*. Composed toward the end of Thomas's life, it breathes an atmosphere of quiet trust and unmistakable confidence. Thomas, aware of the grace of intimacy and fresh hope which prayer can bring, makes an observation which brings into focus something of his own individual practice and understanding of prayer. He writes:

> When we pray to God, the very prayer we send forth makes us intimate with him, inasmuch as our soul is raised up to God, converses with him in spiritual affection, and adores him in spirit and truth. This affectionate intimacy, experienced in prayer, prepares a way to return to prayer with even greater confidence. (2, 2)

St. Thérèse of Lisieux at Prayer

———

I am too small to climb the rough stairway of perfection.

(*Story of a Soul*, Manuscript C, ch. 10)[34]

A few months before she died, Thérèse of Lisieux remarked to one of her spiritual friends: "You don't know me as I really am" (*Letter to l'abbé Bellière*, April 25, 1897). Even today, I imagine, she would say the same thing to anyone unable or unwilling to look beyond the plaster image of the saint, beyond the sweet, beguiling image — that is, of a life perfumed with roses and pious sentiment. Of course, there does exist an undeniable sweetness in the character and writings of Saint Thérèse, but the true history of this "little flower" can sometimes seem more like that of a steel bar than that of a tiny, perfumed rose. This was the belief of Albino Luciano, Blessed John Paul I.[35]

To the suggestion from one of her sisters, Marie of the Sacred Heart, that at the moment of her death she would see angels coming to meet her "resplendent with light and beauty," Thérèse remarked: "All these images do me no good. I can nourish myself on nothing but the truth. That is why I've never wanted any visions."[36] Once, when already in her last months and facing death, she was asked by Mother Agnes (Pauline) "to say a few edifying words" to the doctor attending her, Thérèse's answer was bright and sharp: "Ah! … this isn't my little style. Let Doctor de Cornière think what he wants. I love only simplicity. I have a horror of pretense."[37]

1. A hidden life

Although Thérèse was greatly admired by a small number in her community, to most of the nuns she remained a figure almost unknown. Sister Marie of the Trinity recalls, "During her life in Carmel, the Servant of God passed by unnoticed in the community."[38] Her own blood sister Celine (Sister Geneviève) remarks, "In general, even during her last years, she continued to lead a hidden life, the sublimity of which was known more to God than to the sisters around her" (*Last Conversations*, 18–19).

That even her own blood sisters had little or no insight into the interior life of Saint Thérèse is astonishing, a fact which helps explain the shock Mother Agnes (Pauline) received when she read the initial part of *The Story of a Soul*. No one had read these pages before, a work which, within a few short years, would make a remarkable impact on the Catholic world. Barely able to contain her excitement, Agnes wrote: "This blessed child, who wrote these heavenly pages, is still in our midst! I can speak to her, see her, touch her. Oh! How she is unknown here!" (*Last Conversations*, 22).

Thérèse died on September 30, 1897. She was twenty-four years old. Twenty-eight years later she was canonized, and on October 19, 1997, she was declared a Doctor of the Church. On that occasion Pope John Paul II remarked: "Everyone realizes that today something surprising is happening. St. Thérèse of Lisieux was unable to attend a university or engage in systematic study. She died young: Nevertheless, from this day forward, she will be honored as a Doctor of the Church."[39] But why so honored? John Paul explains, "Her ardent spiritual journey shows such maturity, and the insights of faith expressed in her writings are so vast and profound that they deserve a place among the great spiritual masters."

2. The "little doctrine" of Thérèse

"I want to seek out a means of going to heaven … a way that is very straight, very short, and totally new."
(*Story of a Soul*, Manuscript C, ch. 10, 207)

From a very early age Thérèse desired to be a saint. Her entry into religious life was with the aim, the hope, of fulfilling that desire. Naturally, from the beginning, she looked to the example of the great saints. But Thérèse soon came to realize, and it was a humbling discovery, that she was unable to aim for the highest, most challenging pathways of holiness.

I have always wanted to be a saint. Alas! I have always noticed that when I compared myself to the saints, there is between them and me the same difference that exists between a mountain whose summit is lost in the clouds and the obscure grain of sand trampled underfoot by passers-by. Instead of becoming discouraged, I said to myself: "God cannot inspire unrealizable desires." I can then, in spite of my littleness, aspire to holiness. It is impossible for me to grow up, and so I must bear with myself such as I am with all my imperfections. ... We are living now in an age of inventions, and we no longer have to take the trouble of climbing stairs, for, in the homes of the rich, an elevator has replaced these very successfully. I wanted to find an elevator which would raise me to Jesus. ... I searched then in the Scriptures for some sign of this elevator, the object of my desires, and I read these words coming from the mouth of Eternal Wisdom: "*Whoever is a* LITTLE ONE, *let him come to me.*" And so I succeeded. I felt I found what I was looking for. But wanting to know, O my God, what you would do to *the very little one* who answered your call, I continued my search, and this is what I discovered: "*As one whom his mother comforts, so will I comfort you; you shall be carried at the breast, and upon the knees they will comfort you.*" Ah! Never did words more tender and more melodious come to give joy to my soul. The elevator which must raise me to heaven is your arms, O Jesus! And for this I had no need to grow up, but rather I had to remain *little* and become this more and more. (*Story of a Soul*, Manuscript C, ch. 10)

When asked to describe the "new way" she had discovered, Thérèse replied, "It's the way of spiritual childhood, it's the way of confidence and total surrender" (to Mother Agnes, *Last Conversations*, 257). Thérèse was well aware that she still had faults and failings in her life, but these she was now able to confess, not only with simple candor but also with an astonishing confidence and childlike trust. "I am still weak and imperfect," she writes. "I always feel, however, the same bold confidence of becoming a great saint because I don't count on my merits because I have none. … God alone, content with my weak efforts, will raise me to himself, and make me a saint, clothing me with his infinite merits" (*Story of a Soul*, Manuscript A, ch. 4).

The thought of the stern mortifications of the saints, a form of asceticism of which Thérèse feels wholly incapable, does not in any way make her feel excluded from the path to holiness: "I know there are some saints who spent their life in the practice of astonishing mortifications to expiate their sins, but what of it? 'There are many mansions in the house of my heavenly Father,' Jesus has said, and it is because of this that I follow the way he is tracing out for me" (*Letter to l'abbé Bellière*, June 21, 1887).

This "way," although a path of joy and freedom, does not represent flight from the challenge of the Cross. There is nothing dreamy or escapist, nothing cowardly about it. Thérèse, in one of her poems, writes:

Here on earth, living by love,
is not just pitching a tent on Thabor;
It means climbing Calvary with Jesus,
and looking on the cross as a treasure.

("Vivre d'Amour," in *Thérèse de Lisieux, Oeuvres Complètes*, 667)

Regarding the sources of "the little way," the following question was put to Thérèse by one of the novices, Sister Marie of the Trinity: "Where did this teaching of yours come from?" Thérèse replied: "It is God alone who instructed me. No book, no theologian has taught me" (*Counsels and Memories*, 46).[40] In the past, Thérèse, it appears, had made some effort to communicate her "little way" to others. But those to whom she "opened her soul" failed completely to understand. She "received," she tells Sister Marie, "no encouragement from anyone." It's not difficult, therefore, to imagine the delight Thérèse experienced when she discovered that a respected theologian, the French Dominican Père Boulanger, had been teaching (independently of Thérèse) what appear to be elements of her "little doctrine."

Pages of notes surviving from a retreat which, a few years earlier, the Dominican had given at a different Carmelite monastery, do indeed appear to capture some part of the Thérèsian vision. When eventually Thérèse was made aware by Sister Marie of the ideas contained in these notes, she exclaimed: "What consolation you give me! You can't imagine! To know myself supported by an expert, an eminent theologian, gives me an incomparable joy." Boulanger refers at one point to the apparent "nothings" which make up Carmelite life. But these small "zeros," he says, when joined to God, "the infinite One," become something manifestly graced.[41]

Thérèse was clearly struck by this reflection. A few years later, in a letter to the missionary Père Adolfe Roulland, she chose to refer to herself as 'the little zero' (*Letter to Roulland*, May 9, 1897). Obviously delighted to unite her life and prayer with that of the missionary, she writes: "Let us work together for the salvation of souls. I can do very little, or rather absolutely nothing, if I am alone; what consoles me is to think that at your side I can be useful for something. In fact, zero by itself has no value, but when placed next to a unit it becomes powerful." Powerful indeed! On December 14, 1927, a mere thirty years after her death, Thérèse, who had not even once stepped outside her monastic enclosure, was named by Pope Pius XI the patron saint of foreign missions.

—⟶∿⟵—

The littleness of "the little way" may strike some readers as mere sentimentality, a form of childishness even. But nothing could be further from the truth. To become "little," in Thérèse's understanding, is to have the courage and humility to face the reality of one's life and, with bold, childlike confidence, surrender one's false pride and all other faults and failures to God the Father. "It means," in Thérèse's words, "being ready at heart to become small and humble in the arms of God, acknowledging our own weakness and trusting in His fatherly goodness to the point of audacity."[42]

So impressed was Sister Marie by this teaching of Thérèse, she announced that she was going to share "the little way" with all her relatives and friends "so that they could go straight to heaven."[43] Thérèse, hearing this declaration, felt it necessary to say to Marie that "the little way," if badly explained, could be "taken for quietism." Yes it's true, Jesus is asking simply for "surrender and gratitude," he is not demanding "great actions" (*Story of a Soul*, Manuscript B, ch. 9). Nevertheless, as Pope Francis has tellingly observed, citing Thérèse: "[God] finds few hearts who surrender to him without reservations, few who understand the real tenderness of his infinite love."[44]

As soon as confidence in God and childlike surrender have been established as a new, living part of the saint's or sinner's life, everything changes. Saint and sinner may still be striving, and indeed more than ever, to keep faith with the highest Gospel ideals but, at the same time, they are learning to bear with their faults and failures with more humility, more patience. No longer do they experience a crippling fear of God, nor do they feel shame at simply being human. Such childlike trust in God, such serene confidence, we find manifest again and again in the life of Thérèse, and in a form so audacious at times it can be startling. Thus, for example, towards the end of her life, Thérèse had no hesitation in declaring, "Oh! how happy I am to see myself imperfect and to be so much in need of God's mercy even at the moment of my death!" (Epilogue, *Story of a Soul*, 267).

Hearing a statement of this kind, someone of our own generation who happens to be struggling with weakness, and failing badly, might be inclined to say: "That's amazing, yes, but there is a vast difference between the situation of the young, saintly Thérèse who had lived her whole life in a monastic enclosure, and my own unhappy situation. How can I, with all my sins on my head, dare *with confidence* to go to God?" With these words, the "sinner" might appear to have brought to an abrupt end all possible conversation with the saint.

But Thérèse is not one to be easily put off. Here are a few of her untamed thoughts on the subject: "Mortal sin wouldn't withdraw my confidence from me" (*Last Conversations,* 104). And again: "It is not because God … has preserved my soul from mortal sin that I go to him with confidence. … Even though I had on my conscience all the sins that can be committed, I would go, my heart broken with sorrow, and throw myself into Jesus' arms, for I know how much he loves the prodigal child who returns to him" (*Story of a Soul,* Manuscript C, ch. 9).

3. Prayer in practice

"It is a simple glance directed to heaven; it is a cry of gratitude and love in the midst of trial as well as joy" *(Story of a Soul,* Manuscript C, ch. 9). The simplicity of Thérèse's prayer is one with the simplicity of her life. "I don't have the courage," she notes, "to force myself to search out beautiful prayers in books. There are so many of them it really gives me a headache. … I say very simply to God what I wish to tell him, without composing beautiful sentences, and he always understands me." Books on the spiritual life which she finds unusually dense or complicated, treatises which she can neither understand nor translate into practice, Thérèse is happy to leave to those "great souls" called to pursue perfection in extraordinary ways. But that is not her call. "For simple souls," she writes, "there must be no complicated ways. … I am one of their number."

Initially, it may well have come as a shock to Thérèse to discover she was incapable of following the paths of radical asceticism and high mysticism — the "extraordinary ways" pursued in the past by saints such as John of the Cross and Teresa of Ávila. One detail among others which helped persuade the young Carmelite that her call required a more humble, more "ordinary" way was her decidedly unheroic habit of falling asleep during the time of meditation! Far from becoming upset, however, by this "failure," Thérèse responded with this reflection: "I should be desolate for having slept (for seven years) during my hours of prayer. … Well, I am not desolate … I remember that *the Lord knows our weakness, that he is mindful that we are but dust and ashes*" (ch. 8).

To help keep her focus on God, and also to help her to stay awake at the time of meditation, Thérèse decides to fall back on the humble practice of spiritual reading. But she discovers that even "the most beautiful, the most touching book," makes her heart "contract immediately." In this condition of "helplessness" she turns to Scripture, and to the New Testament in particular. "It is," she writes, "especially the *Gospels* that sustain me during my hours of prayer. … I am constantly discovering in them new lights, hidden and mysterious meaning."

Thérèse refers to "new lights," but there's no hint here of special visions or of any kind of mystical experience. Thérèse has not the least desire for "extraordinary" aids of that kind. With regards to visions, for example, she remarks: "Oh! No! I don't have any desire to see God here on earth. And yet I love him! I also love the Blessed Virgin very much, and the saints, and I don't desire to see them either" (*Last Conversations*, 188). When, in May 1890, her family decided to go on pilgrimage to Lourdes, Thérèse wrote to Sister Agnes: "I have no wish to go to Lourdes to have ecstasies. I prefer the monotony of sacrifice."

So, Thérèse chose not to go in search of Mary at Lourdes — that hallowed place of vision — and instead she searched for Mary, we can say, at Nazareth, and found her there leading a life that was decidedly ordinary: "No raptures, miracles or ecstasies adorned your life. ... You chose, O incomparable Mother, to tread the ordinary way and thus lead little ones to heaven" ("*Pourquoi je t'aime, O Marie!*" in *Oeuvres Complètes*, 754). One saint of the "ordinary way" whom Thérèse particularly admired was a young French missionary, later a canonized saint, Jean-Théophane Venard. Thérèse writes: "Théophane pleases me much more than St. Louis de Gonzague [St. Aloysius Gonzaga] because the life of the latter is extraordinary, and that of Théophane is very ordinary" (*Last Conversations*), adding later: "St. Louis de Gonzague was serious even during recreation, but Théophane was always cheerful."

As examples of bold, childlike trust and simple

prayer, Thérèse looked to two Gospel figures in particular: the publican and Mary Magdalene. "I don't hasten," she writes, "to the first place, but to the last; rather than advance myself like the Pharisee, I repeat, filled with confidence, the publican's humble prayer." Then she adds: "Most of all, I imitate the conduct of Magdalene, her astonishing or rather her loving audacity" (*Story of a Soul*, Manuscript C, ch. 11). Scattered throughout Thérèse's letters, poems, plays, and her celebrated autobiography, are prayers of various kinds, some formal, but the majority free and spontaneous. Over the years, Thérèse prayed not only for her own immediate family and community, she prayed also for sinners. But her prayer for sinners would assume in time a form that no one could have foreseen.

How this came about can best be explained by a series of events described in *Story of a Soul*. Thérèse, having coughed up blood a number of times, realized that she had not long to live. She was, at that time, enjoying "such a living faith, such a *clear* faith" that, rather than being crushed by the news, she was in fact excited at the prospect of soon going to heaven (see ch. 10). But then something happened which changed everything. "[God] permitted my soul," she writes, "to be invaded by the thickest darkness." The thought of heaven, which had been "so sweet" before, was now "the cause of struggle and torment." And "the darkness," Thérèse explains, "borrowing the voice of sinners, says mockingly to me: 'You believe that one day you will walk out of this fog that surrounds you.' But death, the voice goes on to say, will lead you not into light but rather into 'a night still more profound, the night of nothingness.'"

The darkness of spirit which is endured here by Thérèse, with its tremendous anguish, although it may appear identical with the experience described by Christian mystics as the "dark night," achieves something rather different and wholly unexpected: not only a notable transformation in Thérèse's relationship with God, we may presume, but a transformation also in the ways she prays for and relates to sinners, those very "sinners" whose voice she could hear in the night mocking all that was dear to her. It is a startling event of grace. No longer is Thérèse simply praying from *inside* the holy enclosure of Carmel for poor, wretched sinners living out in the world. No, she has now accepted to be placed by God *outside* Carmel, as it were, seated at a table together with "sinners and unbelievers" — her "brothers."

She begs pardon for her brothers and is resigned to eat the bread of sorrow as long as the Lord desires it; she does not wish to rise up from this table filled with bitterness at which poor sinners are eating until the day set by the Lord. Can she not say in her name and in the name of her brothers, "*Have pity on us, Lord, for we are poor sinners?*"

Conclusion

———

Saints, if looked at only from a distance, can appear remote and intimidating, their journey into God following a path that's either too high and mystical or too fiercely ascetic for the ordinary believer. But, although their lives are indeed heroic and exemplary, the saints are the last people to be harshly judgmental of human struggle and human weakness. The saints — the "blessed" in heaven — Thérèse notes in one of her last letters, "have great compassion on our miseries; they remember, being weak and mortal like us; they committed the same faults, sustained the same combats" (*Letter to l'abbé Bellière*, August 10, 1897). This bold declaration of Thérèse helps explain the "bond of union" which has always existed in Christianity between saint and sinner. "The sinner," writes Charles Péguy, "holds out a hand to the saint, gives a hand to the saint, since the saint gives a hand to the sinner. And all together, one by means of the other, one pulling up the other, they ascend to Jesus" ("The Christian Life," in *Basic Verities*, 181–83).

Hearing, overhearing, four celebrated saints at prayer in this brief study — Augustine, Teresa, Thomas, and Thérèse — has been a revelation. All four saints, although inspired by the same Christian faith, and similar in many ways, are also astonishingly diverse in character and style, all four wonderfully able to bring to their reflections on prayer the freshness of the new and the surprise of the Gospel. The fact of their diversity, the many striking differences between them, carries a message, I would suggest, of no small importance for our own lives today, a message expressed centuries ago by Teresa of Ávila: "God doesn't lead us all by one path, and perhaps the one who thinks she is walking along a very lowly path is, in fact, higher in the ways of the Lord" (*The Way of Perfection*, ch. 17, 2).

One of the saints who made an enormous impact on the life of Saint Thérèse was her fellow Carmelite, the Spanish mystic and poet John of the Cross. Thérèse deeply revered John, but so "extraordinary" in her view was his ascetical and mystical path that she realized she would need to find for herself a different path to God, a more "ordinary" way. She would not be setting out, therefore, like a hero, to ascend the impossibly high Mountain of Carmel. No, she would *descend*, as it were, and with the humility and simplicity of a child would fall back into the arms of Jesus, trusting him with complete confidence to bring her gradually to the heights of union. It was this "little way" which, in time, Thérèse felt called to communicate to others. Here, for example, touching directly on her "*petite voie*," is a down-to-earth piece of advice offered by Thérèse to one of her sisters: "You are wanting to climb up a high mountain, but the good God wants you to descend; he is waiting for you at the bottom of the fertile valley of humility."[45]

Thérèse, on occasion, cites individual lines and phrases from both the poetry and prose of St. John of the Cross. One text, among others, which caught her attention, and to which she refers a number of times, is a short prose meditation entitled "Prayer of a Soul Taken with Love." Sister Geneviève tells us that this prayer filled Thérèse with joy and hope. And it's easy to see why. It expresses a conviction about being loved by God with an audacity to match Thérèse's own. But that is not, as it happens, how the prayer begins. The opening few sentences introduce us to a man clearly troubled by the thought that God may still be remembering his past "sins" or may perhaps have noticed the lack of sufficient "good works" in his life. But, if these things are not the problem, what is the reason for God's "delay"?

> What is it that makes you wait, my most clement Lord? Why do you delay? For if, after all, I am to receive the grace and mercy which I entreat of you in your Son, take my mite, since you desire it, and grant me this blessing, since you also desire that. Who can free himself from lowly

manners and limitations if you do not lift him to yourself, my God, in purity of love? How will a man begotten and nurtured in lowliness rise up to you, Lord, if you do not raise him with your hand which made him?[46]

While still in a state of manifest distress — fully conscious of his need for compassion — John, all of a sudden, remembers Christ, the Son of God, and that changes everything. The prayer of the sinner becomes at once the prayer of a saint. John is no longer haunted by the sins and failures of his past. On the contrary, because of Christ's love he finds he is now able to breathe deep with a new confidence and a new joy. I can think of no better way of bringing to a close this brief reflection on saints and sinners at prayer than by continuing Saint John's radiant words:

> You will not take from me, my God, what you once gave me in your only Son, Jesus Christ, in whom you gave me all I desire. Hence, I rejoice that if I wait for you, you will not delay. With what procrastinations do you wait [my soul], since from this very moment you can love God in your heart? Mine are the heavens and mine is the earth. Mine are the nations, the just are mine, and mine the sinners. The angels are mine, and the Mother of God, and all things are mine; and God himself is mine and for me, because Christ is mine and all for me.

Notes

[1] *The Nine Ways of Prayer of Saint Dominic*. Translated and edited by Simon Tugwell (Dublin: Dominican Publications, 1978), 18.

[2] Teresa of Ávila, *The Interior Castle, The Collected Works*, vol. 2. Translated by Kieran Kavanaugh and Otilio Rodriguez (Washington: ICS Publication, 1987), 443.

[3] Vincent McNabb, *The Craft of Prayer* (London: Sheed and Ward, 1935), 77.

[4] *The Anonymous Sayings of the Desert Fathers, Apophthegmata Patrum*, Translated by Simon Tugwell in *The Way of the Preacher* (London: Darton, Longman, and Todd, 1979), 137–38.

[5] *The Life of St. Teresa of Avila by Herself*, Translated by JM Cohen (London: Penguin, 1957), 69.

[6] Augustine, *The Confessions*, Translated by R. P. Pine-Coffin (London: Hammondsworth, 1961), 43.

[7] *Expositions of the Psalms*, 6 volumes, Maria Boulding (New York: Horizon, 2000-2004).

[8] Benedict XVI, Meeting with the Seminarians of the Major Roman Seminary, February 17, 2007.

[9] Augustine on Psalm 36:3, cited in Hugh Pope, *St. Augustine of Hippo* (New York: Image, 1961), 106.

[10] Sermon 114, 4, *Sermons on the New Testament*, in *The Works of Saint Augustine*, Part III, Translated by Edmund Hill (New York: New City Press, 1991), 189.

[11] John Henry Newman, "Sins of Infirmity," Sermon 15, in *Parochial and Plain Sermons*, vol. 5 (London: Longmans, Green, 1891), 212–23.

[12] Benedict XVI, General Audience, January 16, 2008.

[13] Benedict XVI, Encounter with Seminarians of the Roman Major Seminary, February 17, 2007.

[14] Teresa of Ávila, "Soliloquies," *The Collected Works*, vol. 1, 447.

[15] Jerónimo Gracián *La Peregrinación de Anastasio* (Santa Barbara, California: Santa Barbara Publications of eHumanista, 2021). See also Erika Lorenz, *Teresa of Ávila and Father Gracián: The Story of an Historic Friendship* (Leominster, UK: Gracewing, 2012), 82.

[16] Teresa of Ávila, "Spiritual Testimonies," *The Collected Works*, vol. 1, 393.

[17] B. Foreshow, *The New Catholic Encyclopedia*, vol. 4 (Washington, 1967), 938–39.

[18] Paul VI, Homily on the Occasion of the *Proclamation of Saint Teresa of Ávila, Doctor of the Church*, September 27, 1970.

[19] Teresa of Ávila, *The Book of Her Life, The Collected Works*, vol. 1, 252.

[20] *The Collected Works*, vol. 2, 115.

[21] *The Life of Saint Teresa by Herself*, 63.

[22] Thomas Aquinas, Prayer for Forgiveness, in *S. Thomae Aquinatis opuscula theologica*, vol. 1, Marietti edition (Rome, 1954), 289.

[23] *The Lectures on St. Matthew*, in *Albert and Thomas: Selected Writings*, Translated and edited by Simon Tugwell (New York: Paulist, 1988), 470–71.

[24] A. G. Sertillanges, *Prières de Saint Thomas d'Aquin* (Paris, 1920), 8. On the debates regarding the question of Aquinas's

authorship, see the latest (2023) edition of Jean-Pierre Torrell's *Saint Thomas Aquinas: The Person and the Work*, 154–58 and 429–30.

[25] Claire le Brun-Goanvic, *Ystoria sancti Thome de Aquino de Guillaume de Tocco*, 29 (Toronto: Pontifical Institute of Mediaeval Studies, 1996), 156; P. Murray, *Aquinas at Prayer: The Bible, Mysticism, and Poetry* (London: Bloomsbury Continuum, 2013), 32–4. *Adoro Te Devote*, although often sung as a hymn, was composed originally as a prayer.

[26] A phrase of Aquinas in his commentary on Psalm 39:2. See *In psalmos Davidis expositio*, Parma edition, vol. 14, 300.

[27] Prayer for Wise Ordering (*Concede michi*). Translated by Paul Murray, O.P.

[28] *Compendium theologiae*, in *Leonine Critical edition of the Opera omnia*, vol. 42 (Rome: Commissio Leonina, 1979).

[29] Thomas Aquinas, in *Orationem Dominicam, expositio* no. 1034, 223.

[30] *Super primam epistolam ad Timotheum lectura*, ch. 2, lect. 1, 56, *Super epistolas s. Pauli lectura*, vol. 2, 224.

[31] *Super epistolam ad Hebraeos lectura*, ch. 5, lect. 1, in *Super epistolas*, vol. 2, 390.

[32] Thomas Aquinas, Prologue, 6, *Super epistolas s. Pauli lectura*, Marietti edition.

[33] In Psalmos 56:5, Busa edition, vol. 6, 128.

[34] *Story of a Soul: The Autobiography of St. Thérèse de Lisieux*, Translated by John Clarke (Washington: ICS Publications, 1996), 207.

[35] See Albino Luciano (Blessed John Paul I), *Illustrissimi: Letters from Pope John Paul I* (Boston: Little, Brown, and Co., 1978), 146.

36 *Thérèse* to Sister Marie of the Sacred Heart, August 5, 1897, *Her Last Conversations*, John Clarke (Washington, 1997) 134.

37 Comment of *Thérèse* to Mother Agnes on July 7, 1897, *Last Conversations*, 77.

38 Sister Marie of the Trinity, Witness 17, Acts of the Ordinary Process 1910–11 (Carmelite archives).

39 John Paul II, *Proclamation of St. Thérèse as a Doctor of the Church*, October 19, 1997.

40 *Conseils et souvenirs de Marie de la Trinité*, no. 46 (Carmelite archives).

41 See sermon of P. Boulanger in Pierre Descouvemont, *Thérèse of Lisieux and Marie of the Trinity* (New York: Alba House, 1997), 28–9.

42 *Novissima verba*, cited in Hans Urs von Balthasar, *Two Sisters in the Spirit*: Thérèse *of Lisieux and Elizabeth of the Trinity* (San Francisco: Ignatius, 1992), 243.

43 Testimony of Sister Marie of the Trinity from the Process for Beatification, See *Thérèse of Lisieux By Those Who Knew Her* (Dublin: Veritas, 1975), 235–36.

44 Pope Francis, Homily at Mikheil Meskhi Stadium, Tbolisi, Georgia, October 1, 2016.

45 *Conseils et souvenirs de Marie de la Trinité* (Carmelite archives).

46 John of the Cross, Prayer of a Soul Taken with Love, in *The Collected Works*. Translated by Kieran Kavanaugh and Otilio Rodriguez (Washington: ICS Publications, 1991), 668–69.

Available at
OSVCatholicBookstore.com
or wherever books are sold

In preparation for the Jubilee Year 2025, the Exploring Prayer series delves into the various dimensions of prayer in the Christian life. These brief, accessible books can help you learn to dialogue with God and rediscover the beauty of trusting in the Lord with humility and joy.

Prayer Today: A Challenge to Overcome
Notes on Prayer: Volume 1
by Angelo Comastri
In order to have saints, what is needed are people of authentic prayer, and authentic prayer is that which inflames with a fire of love. Only in this way is it possible to lift the world and bring it near to the heart of God. To pray in truth, we must present ourselves before God with the open wounds of our smallness and our sin. Only in this way will the encounter with God be an encounter of liberation and redemption.

Praying with the Psalms
Notes on Prayer: Volume 2
by Gianfranco Ravasi
This little guide to the Psalms includes four cardinal points: a general reflection on prayer, the breath of the soul; a panoramic look at the psalmic texts; a portrait of the two protagonists, God and the worshipper, but also the intrusion of the presence of evil; and finally, an anthology of brief commentaries on the Psalms most dear to tradition and the liturgy. The hope is that all the faithful may draw fully from this wonderful treasury of prayers.

The Jesus Prayer
Notes on Prayer: Volume 3
by Juan Lopez Vergara
This book explores the unique experience of the fatherhood of God for Jesus Christ, whom he calls Abba — which in his native Aramaic language means "Dad." Throughout his earthly life, Jesus is in contact dialogue with Abba. From his Baptism in the Jordan through his public ministry and ultimately his crucifixion, this relationship will mark him forever, transforming his life, and our lives, too.

Praying with Saints and Sinners
Notes on Prayer: Volume 4
by Paul Brendan Murray
The saints whose writings on prayer and meditation

are explored in this book are among the most celebrated in the great spiritual tradition. The aim of this book is to discover what help the great saints can offer those of us who desire to make progress in the life of prayer, but who find ourselves being constantly deflected from our purpose, our tentative efforts undermined perhaps most of all by human weakness.

Parables on Prayer
Notes on Prayer: Volume 5
by Anthony Pitta
What characterizes, in a singular way, Jesus's teaching on prayer is the recourse to parables. Jesus did not invent a new system for praying. Jesus was not a hermit, a Buddhist monk, or a yogi. He instead chose the daily life of his people to teach prayer with parables. This book explores the parables in the Gospels explicitly related to prayer. The reader is guided by Jesus, the original teacher of prayer with parables.

The Church in Prayer
Notes on Prayer: Volume 6
by Carthusian Monks
Carthusian Monks reside in several international monasteries. Founded in 1084 by Saint Bruno, the Order of Carthusians are dedicated to prayer, in silence, in community. Like other cloistered religious, the Carthusians live a life focused on prayer and contemplation.

The Prayer of Mary and the Saints
Notes on Prayer: Volume 7
by Catherine Aubin

When Mary appears, anywhere in the whole world, the places where she appears have points in common with the biblical places where she stayed and lived. This book reviews these places, examining what they reveal to us about Mary's identity, and what the inner spaces are that Mary asks us to dwell in today. This book also explores the unique relationship two holy women each had with Mary, leading us toward a new, deep revelation of Mary's closeness to each of us.

The Prayer Jesus Taught Us: The "Our Father"
Notes on Prayer: Volume 8
by Hugh Vanni

This book identifies the theological-biblical structure underlying the Lord's Prayer and situates it in the living environment of the early Church. This will give us a framework of reference, and as a result we will see first the antecedents in Mark, then the systematic presentation of Matthew, Paul's push forward, the accentuation of Luke, and, finally, the mature synthesis found in John.